Overnight

Also by the author

Poetry:

Waterworks
In Baltic Circles
Harmatan
Some Poems
Splurge
Likewise
The Curious Builder
The Anamorphosis
Fracas
Breakers

Prose:

Selected Accidents, Pointless Anecdotes

Overnight

Paul Violi

Hanging Loose Press
Brooklyn, New York

Published by Hanging Loose Press
231 Wyckoff Street
Brooklyn, NY 11217-2208.
www.hangingloosepress.com

Printed in the United States of America
10 9 8 7 6 5 4 3 2 1

Hanging Loose Press thanks the Literature Program of the New York State Council on the Arts for a grant in support of the publication of this book.

Some of these poems previously appeared in the following publications: *Blackbox, Deliberately Thirsty, Green Mountains Review, Goodfoot, Tears in the Fence, Oar, Barrow Street, Poetry Quarterly Review, Lit, Terrible Work, Shiny, Poetry Daily, The Mississippi Review, Ploughshares, Sal Mimeo, MIPOesias, /seconds, The Next Chapter: Poem-a-Day, The World, The Columbia Review, The North, Hanging Loose, Aphros, The Blue and White, Poetry Project Newsletter, Exultations and Difficulties, Alhambra Poetry Calendar 2006, Pataphysics.*

Several poems also appeared in the anthologies *Best American Poetry 2000, 2004* and *2006, Poetry After 9/11: An Anthology of New York Poets, The Blind See Only This World, 180 More, Great American Prose Poems: From Poe to the Present,* and *The Oxford Book of American Poetry.*

Envoy and many of the poems in *For a February Songbook* were published in two art book collaborations with Dale Devereux Barker: *Gris Gris* and *Envoy; Life Is Completely Interesting.*

Library of Congress Cataloging-in-Publication Data available on request.

ISBN: 978-1-931236-78-2 (paper)
ISBN: 978-1-931236-79-9 (cloth)

Produced at The Print Center, Inc., 225 Varick St., New York, NY 10014, a non-profit facility for literary and arts-related publications. (212) 206-8465

Contents

I. Overnight

II. For a February Songbook

To David and Alexandra Kelley

I Overnight

Appeal to the Grammarians

We, the naturally hopeful,
Need a simple sign
For the myriad ways we're capsized.
We who love precise language
Need a finer way to convey
Disappointment and perplexity.
For speechlessness and all its inflections,
For up-ended expectations,
For every time we're ambushed
By trivial or stupefying irony,
For pure incredulity, we need
The inverted exclamation point.
For the dropped smile, the limp handshake,
For whoever has just unwrapped a dumb gift
Or taken the first sip of a flat beer,
Or felt love or pond ice
Give way underfoot, we deserve it.
We need it for the air pocket, the scratch shot,
The child whose ball doesn't bounce back,
The flat tire at journey's outset,
The odyssey that ends up in Weehawken.
But mainly because I need it—here and now
As I sit outside the Caffe Reggio
Staring at my espresso and cannoli
After this middle-aged couple
Came strolling by and he suddenly
Veered and sneezed all over my table
And she said to him, "See, *that's* why
I don't like to eat outside."

Finish These Sentences

The qualities I look for in a subordinate are

A situation in which humor might be most unwelcome is

After considering which is better, to be wealthy or wise

My greatest sense of personal fulfillment depends on

It's one thing to champion a sticky empiricism
But it's another altogether different thing to

I think of myself as a caring professional who as the days
And nights tumble by like woozy pandas trying to achieve
A position conducive to procreation

She had an accent that turned eyes to ice, heart
to hard, and transubstantiation to

From the bloody throats of those dull-colored birds
That scream at the sun,

As a patch of grass and wildflowers where lovers lay
Begins to revive, so too my mind once oppressed by joy

In that one moment when they begin to flap
Frantically in their doomed arc, the great books I fling
Off a high balcony almost

A complete individual is one who

Now there are hands, lovely hands that have played
Rare instruments in the dark and thrown
Many a burning basket into the wind, and there are eyes

I like to think my superiors value my ability to

It is easy for me first thing in the morning to scoff
At questions like how many angels can dance on a pinhead,
But such figments, especially when immersed in paradox,
Oxymora and the like, don't seem so frivolous when we
Recollect the most intense and memorable experiences of our
Lives, experiences that in one moment produce a state of
Devastating superflux, of many simultaneous, powerful and
Distinct if not contradictory feelings, that when captured
In words not only allow the closest thing to prayer that the
Faithless can rely on for solace, but also remind us how
Figurative speech provides a refined atavistic satisfaction,
Especially evident in the way deeply imagined metaphor by
Enlivening objects reawakens the residual susceptibility
Of the primitive, superstitious mind to fetishism and

As I Was Telling Dave and Alex Kelley

My brother swears this is true.
And others have willingly—
generously testified,
As they did that other time when
After leaving an office party
They pulled off the expressway,
Walked into a place he'd never
Been to before, and ordered
A few more drinks while he
Headed for the lavatory.
But as he was crossing the dining room
On the other side of the bar
This vicious fight broke out.
Two women—well-dressed, tall,
Gorgeous—tore into each other,
Punching, clawing, swinging
Spike-heeled shoes, pulling
Each other's hair, and my brother,
Aghast, jumped between them
To break it up, grabbed them roughly,
Held them apart, berated
Them, tried to shake some sense
Into—when he gradually pieced
It all together: the changed look
On their faces, the disapproval,
The utter silence of condemnation
That everyone aimed not at the women
But at him, the fact that
It was a supper club theatre
And he had just jumped into
The climactic scene of a play—
But this, I hasten to add, is not
About my brother but his neighbor,
A man whose roof needed repair;

A man who, more than most, feared heights.
A ladder to this neighbor
Didn't ordinarily suggest the kind
Of elevating work that joins
The material to the spiritual,
So before mounting it he called
His children over and, as he wrapped
A rope thick enough to moor a barge
Around his waist and lashed
The other end around the car bumper,
Carefully explained to them
How they should steady the ladder
Until he had climbed onto the roof.
Up he went, not overstepping
But securing both feet on the same rung
Before proceeding to the next:
A trembling man on a trembling ladder.
He squirmed over the drain,
Crawled up the not very steep slope,
Flopped over the peak, then slid
Inch by inch down the rear slope
Until he felt confident enough
To kneel instead of crawl,
To sigh and take a deep breath
Before he began to cut a shingle.
Perhaps the first horripilating signal
Was a subtle tug on the rope,
Like an angel plucking a harp string.
Perhaps it was a sudden tautness
Around his waist, or, perhaps,
He heard the station wagon door
Slam shut, then the ignition,
The engine roar to life, or
Slowly grindingly churn before it
Kicked in and he was yanked heavenward
Then jerked back, slammed, twisted,
Keelhauled belly up, belly down,
Over the roof, dashed onto the driveway

To be dragged, dribbled,
Bounced hard along the road, his
Wife looking this way and that
As she drove on, wondering
Wherever were those screams coming from?
Doctors, police, all believed
She could very well have not seen
The rope; could not, with windows   .
Rolled up, have ascertained,
While they lasted, the source,
Proximity and intensity of the screams.
And I, for one, though respectful
Of the family's desire for privacy,
Think for numerous, inevitable,
Irresistible philosophical,
Sociological but mostly religious
Reasons, this place, this event,
This man deserves a shrine
Which, if donations are forthcoming,
I am willing to oversee
The construction of
At 145 Sampson Avenue,
Islip, Long Island, New York.
That's right, that's the name
Of the place: Islip. I swear.

A Podiatrist Crawls Home in the Moonlight

Right knee left foot
Left knee right foot
Right ouch
Asphalt

Elbow knee
Elbow foot
Knee foot
Foot slip
Face hurt

Asphalt grass
Forearm dirt
Ooof ouch
Brickwork

Nudge shrub
Bush clutch
Flowerbed
Rose white
Nose cool

Backdoor
Doorknob
Tall grass
Sweet grass
Flop floof
Gasp sigh

Pants pocket
No key
Pants pocket
No key

Suit pocket
No key

Tie flip
Damp stain
Sniff silk
Whiff
Oil

Sniff silk
Whiff champagne
Whiff...gunpowder?
Whiff-whiff
Gunpowder

Bug pile
Lamplight
Broken wings
Broken bugs

Sniff sky
Sniff and decide
Freedom
Beauty
Sniff and decide

Freedom and beauty
And the fleet-footed pursuit
Of essential thrills
Are the key
To good health and happiness.

I.D.

Or, Mistaken Identities

1.

To the island of my birth I returned
And spent my days
Taking life a thought at a time.
But no sooner would I squash
The life out of one thought
Than another jumped in.
Where did it get me,
A blind old man on the docks,
Staring beyond the sound of waves,
Pestering fishermen for stories,
Any story of the sea?
Hearing boys ship their oars,
Curse their snagged nets,
I asked them, "How did it go?
What did you catch?"
Only to have some wiseacre
Toss a riddle at me:
"We threw away what we caught.
What we didn't catch,
We kept them all."
That shut me up, stumped
By a couple of twerps.
For the life of me
I couldn't figure it out.
I mean trying to figure it out was
What did me in. I trudged off,
Scratching my bald head,
Looking like a scowling fool.
Distracted, I slipped on the slick bank
And down I went, busted up on the rocks.
I survived for a few more days,
Still wondering.

Who am I?

2.

For sixty-two years my mother
Carried me in her womb, so
It was not very strange
That I was born with white hair,
Nor that thereafter
I always endeavored
To conceal myself from the world.
I became a librarian.
Years of scholarship led me
To believe that people
Should be firmly ruled
By benevolent sages.
I advocated simplicity,
Compassion, spontaneity
And obscurity
As the greatest virtues
And concluded that the best way
To live was to do
Nothing but remain pure and still.
I sought transformation.
Dismayed by corruption and disorder,
I decided to wander off
Into the outlands.
At my departure, the gatekeeper
Importuned me to write down my thoughts,
Which I did, spontaneously,
Producing a short,
Extraordinarily obscure book
On the greatness of little things.
No one heard from me again;
Countless millions have pondered my book.

Who am I?

3.

For handing over Philologus
To the widow of the man
I'd commanded him to murder
(She then made him slice off bits
Of his own flesh, roast them
And then eat them)—For this,
Plutarch commended me
For at least one act
Of understanding and decency.

Who am I?

4.

My training as a magician was ordinary:
Rigorous and unpleasant.
I performed various ceremonies
. Mostly of a religio-sexual nature
To promote fishing and cultivation.
I fostered vague beliefs in an array
Of powerful beings, most of whom
Were mischievous and stupid.
Transmigration into animals
Was my specialty.
It was a demanding job:
The spirits of my ancient ancestors
Control such practices but,
A cantankerous lot, they
Often withheld their favors.
I left my body after I died
And traveled to an unknown western isle
Where to my relief
There were no deities,
Nor any conception of one, for that matter.
These days I return occasionally
To my former homeland
To marry a gorgeous mortal.
My nickname is "Frizzy."

Who am I?

5.

I always promised less
Than I knew I could deliver.
I made every favor
A surprise or a tribute.
I always greeted the mighty
With what they needed:
A look of wonder.
I studied the lives of the great caliphs:
He whose harem was guarded
By 8,000 eunuchs, half of them
White, half of them black;
He who poured a thousand pearls
Over the head of his first bride;
He who used infants' skulls for candle-snuffers;
He who founded a wondrous city
Centered on the garden
Of a Christian hermit named Dad.
Not for nothing was I made vizier—
Vizier to the Fatamite Caliph Aziz,
He who craved Baalbec cherries
More than the most virile believers
Stranded in a waste of sand
Yearn for unmentionable things.
For him I ordered a flock of 600 pigeons
To be dispatched from Baalbec to Cairo,
Each of which carried attached
To either leg a little silk bag
Containing a cherry.
Eventually, I was slain by infidels
Who buried my head in a pigskin sack.

Who am I?

6.

I set my heart on serving my Lord,
So that to Paradise I could ascend,
That holy place where, so I'd heard,
The fun, the games and laughter never end.

Without my honey, I couldn't go there.
Separated from her, I'd only be sad.
She with the lovely face, the golden hair,
Without her there's no joy to be had.

But I don't mean this to sound so willful,
As if I'd risked eternal damnation.
I didn't *have* to see her beautiful
Figure, or have her soft glance fall on me.
I just prayed for a little consolation:
To see her standing there in all her glory.

Who am I?

7.

Taddeo Bernardi of Lucca
Invited me to supper.
He was wealthy but ridiculous,
A show-off, a big galoot.
I no sooner arrived than,
As if inducting me into paradise,
He showed me a great room
Where luxuriant tapestries
Hung above a floor made
Of colorful stones laid
In the most intricate pattern
Of vines, branches and leaves.
I gazed around, admiring everything,
And then spit in his face.
He was flabbergasted and deeply hurt.
In a not insensitive tone of voice
I hastened to explain:
"I didn't know where else to spit
That would have offended you less."

Who am I?

8.

To repair my health
And our fellowship,
To help me overcome
What he called
My "self-indulgences,"
My dearest friend invited me
To join him and his sister
On a journey, a tour
To remote parts of Scotland.
At the time, I dreaded sleep.
The nightmares that terrified me
Were more vivid than anything
I saw with open eyes.
Suffering from addiction,
In love with a woman
I could never possess,
Dejected, jealous
Of my friend's accomplishment
Whilst my own creative power waned,
Estranged from him
And everyone I loved
…Mayhap, I should not have agreed
To accompany them.
We sat back to back on benches
That ran the length
Of an open carriage,
A laughable equipage yanked
About by a swayback mare.
It rained and rained and I had
To listen helplessly
To his irrepressible sister,
Who, thinking to lift
All our spirits, recited
His verses for mile upon mile.
We parted ways.
With little money, no change

Of clothes, and poor shoes,
This wayward sample of mortality
Walked 263 miles in eight days.
One night during that time,
Somewhere—O somewhere!—
In the company of strangers,
Suffering from hunger,
Bloody feet, hysterical fits,
Uncontrollable weeping,
Stomach pains, dreams
Of shame and terror,
I resolved to marry
My philosophical investigations
To the daily thrills and fears
Of my own extinction, and thus
Engender and engild the great book of my life!

Who am I?

9.

Try this on for size:
I'm driving, o.k.? I'm tired.
Busted muffler's shaking my teeth loose.
I worked late. Too much coffee.
Way too much coffee, o. k.?
I finally get home, o.k.?
I nod hello to the wife.
I'm standing in front of the TV.
You know what I mean,
Standing there, flipping channels.
But then there's this close-up,
A moon-faced kid lying on a floor, o.k.?
Her whole face fills the screen.
I mean, she's right there, jabbing away
At an electronic keyboard
With her tongue.
Her head's bobbing along
Up and down, back and forth
And she's poking hard
At the wet keys under her chin.
The camera moves back and so do I.
Don't get me wrong,
I wasn't frightened.
Hell, I was in Korea *and* 'Nam,
So you know what I mean, o.k.?
She's lying on a blue rug,
She's wearing a blue jumpsuit,
The studio's red, white and blue,
But she's got no arms or legs
And she's going fierce and crazy
Playing the Star Spangled Banner.
The audience is standing around her.
They're looking down, jaws hanging,
Hands folded, really quiet.
They don't know what to think, o.k.?
They're glancing at the m.c.
Hoping he'll tip them off, o.k.?

Then there's a close-up of the m.c.
There he is, Morton Downey, Jr.
Tears are spilling from his eyes
And running down his facial warts, o.k.?
This is a delicate moment.
The crescendo's building
And so is the suspense.
This babe, at any moment she might lean
Too far into that last
Screeching note and turn turtle.
You know what I mean: belly up!
I can't take it, it's not just the coffee, o.k.?
I want to flee out the back door
Of the Home of the Brave.
I got to change channels.
I get this, I get that,
I get static, I get fuzz,
I get vertical horizontals.
Then I get a black and white re-run.
Here's this guy running out a back door,
Down an alley, into a street.
He's amazed at the sight
Of normal-looking people, o.k.?
He's dressed in futurismo leotards,
They're dressed regular.
He's a waylaid earthling, o.k.?
He keeps grabbing them:
"Quick! You've got to tell me,
Where am I? What planet is this?"
That's it, the show's over!
Just like that.
So I turn to the wife and say,
Is that how it ends?
All she wants to do is get drunk
And watch *Lost Weekend* again.
But I really want to know,
Is that how it ends?

Who am I?

10.

I was fired today by a man with a terrible stutter.
His name was Garcia and—clean-cut,
Starched white shirt, bland tie,
The look of a conniving altar boy—
I couldn't help but like him.
The news surprised me.
I thought he intended
To offer congratulations
For a couple of fortunate
Events that had befallen me.
But since I didn't need the job
I quickly regained my equanimity.
He, as usual, was quite tense.
So to proceed smoothly,
Not to say sympathetically,
And to try to put him at ease
I began to help him pronounce
Those words that were proving
Particularly troublesome.
At first I attempted to coax him along
With charade-like gestures,
But the more I tried to help
The more help he needed,
And I was soon completing phrases
For him, then supplying entire sentences.
This reached an unforseen result:
I realized that I had fired myself,
Not "for ca-ca-ca-cause,
Buh-buh-buh-but puh-puh-puh-pol—"
"Policy?"
"Yes, puh-puh-puh-puh-pol—"
"Policy!"
When we agreed that the meeting
Had probably come to an end,
We both rose a little hesitantly
From our chairs, leaned

toward each other over his desk
And almost shook hands.
I left, feeling sorry that, for some reason,
I'd always made that fellow nervous.

Who am I?

11.

I seemed so likeable, so pleasant.
Everyone agreed.
In truth, I smelled like an old leper.
I was a vile, scrawny coward
Who with my armor off or on
Had to be propped up
So I wouldn't fall and drown
Face down in a puddle.

I can't explain my renown.
Indeed, more than once
I left the battlefield
Wondering who had won
And what was lost.

I was either a stingy and nasty
Or a wildly generous host.
Whenever I went broke
I'd sell more land
To have more fun
With my freeloading troubadour pals.

Though I often didn't know
Who or where I was, debtors
Had no trouble finding me
If they had a good ear
—and a thirst!

I could never decide
What to call
The kinds of poems I wrote,
Never knew
What I was saying.
They were more
Of a mystery to me
Than I was to myself.

Though Marcabru
Saluted me,
And the great Peire d'Alvernhe,
I suffered fools
Whose praise left me
Unable to see
Anything better
In a mirror
Than a raw oyster
On a sun-baked rock.

But when lovely words
Caught me in a rush
Of music glad and bold,
Like birds burst into flight,
Like a fountain blown—like
A tree I once saw
(I don't know what kind)
Whose leaves—as heavy as velvet,
As soft and light
As a delicate hand—
Whose dark leaves
With their bright undersides
Burst upward in a wayward gust,
All I could say was
I exceed myself.

I sent my little birds to play
In the fount of all my grief and mirth,
Noble ladies whose replies
Bludgeoned me with subtleties.

Without ever having seen her, I fell
In love with one, the Countess of Urgell.
The poems I sent her
Every summer day and winter
Night, somehow convinced her
Of my worth.

But now—look at this!
Whatever it is, fast or slow
I've managed to finish it
Without an ending or a worry.

I wrote it without knowing
Where it was going
Or whether it was written
For the many or the few
Or the one (who

Could turn a vague joke
Into a sweet little mystery.
The one who
Long after her husband
Died, long after she became a nun,
Said her one regret
Was that she never let
Me touch her bare leg
With the back of my hand).

Who am I?

Acknowledgments

The author wishes to express his profound gratitude to the following publications in which some of these works previously appeared: *Architectural Digest*: "This Lime-Tree Bower My Prison"; *Teen Life*: "On the Death of Chatterton"; *Cosmopolitan*: "Constancy to an Ideal Object"; *Bon Appetit*: "Drinking versus Thinking," "The Eagle and the Tortoise"; *La Cucina Italiana*: "Fire, Famine and Slaughter"; *House Beautiful*: "Kublai Khan," "This Lime-Tree Bower My Prison"; *Better Homes and Gardens*: "This Lime-Tree Bower My Prison," "Reflections on Having Left a Place of Retirement," "Fears in Solitude," "Dejection: an Ode"; *Modern Bride*: "The Rime of the Ancient Mariner"; *American Bride*: "A Lover's Complaint to His Mistress Who Deserted Him In Quest of a More Wealthy Husband in the East Indies"; *Mechanics Illustrated*: "Work Without Hope"; *Popular Mechanics*: "Work Without Hope"; *Interiors*: "Kublai Khan"; *Sports Illustrated*: "Dejection: an Ode"; *Hustler*: "Christabel."

STANZA

The moss is withered, the gardens are lost,
    The noon air fades to a sallow haze,
The lakes lie low under pollen and dust,
    The fields look crushed
As though smothered by floods,
    The lawns are dead, the woods
Are still, the stream bed dry,
    And, like a great bell cast
From summer's weight and solitude's,
    Thunder rocks a cloudless sky.

Pisa, 1822

To Dante Alighieri

from Cecco Angiolieri

Dante, if I'm a lout, you're a lummox.
I mooch a snack, you barge into a feast.
I act snooty, you play the gaudy snob.
I pluck a sonnet out of the gutter,
You dump a new canto in Faeryland.
I'm amazed you haven't caught on by now:
I stay skinny to make you look fatter.
But competition makes us both losers.
You sound more like a blowhard and you're so
Easy to beat the game's become a bore.
I fear you might perform the miracle
That would wring the fun out of all my sins.
So, let's call it a draw. If not, think twice:
As the mud deepens, who's the gadfly…who the ox?

In Khlebnikov's Aviary

O you Cacklers, cackle away!
 O Cacklers and Cacklettes,
          cackle cackle cackle!

Arise, O Ridicules, O righteous Cacklings,
   snicker and snigger, cackle and gloat!
Cackleladies and Cacklegents,
    cackling cackleophonously,
               O my Cackleeeeers!

Greet the morn, O you Cacklers and Cacklettes!
           Weclome Chuckleheads,
Welcome to Cackledom!
   O you cacklelishly contagious Cacklings!
Splattering cachinnations, cackle every which way!
        Cease not, O noontide Cacklettes
            and Cacklings—cackle away!

Cackle away all ye Cacklers,
       O Cacklings and Cacklettes,
                  Cackle away!

COUNTERMAN

What'll it be?

Roast beef on rye, with tomato and mayo.

Whaddaya want on it?

A swipe of mayo.
Pepper but no salt.

You got it. Roast beef on rye.
You want lettuce on that?

No. Just tomato and mayo.

Tomato and mayo. You got it.
...Salt and pepper?

No salt, just a little pepper.

You got it. No salt.
You want tomato.

Yes. Tomato. No lettuce.

No lettuce. You got it.
...No salt, right?

Right. No salt.

You got it. Pickle?

No, no pickle. Just tomato and mayo.
And pepper.

Pepper.

Yes, a little pepper.

Right. A little pepper.
No pickle.

Right. No pickle.

You got it.
Next!

Roast beef on whole wheat, please,
With lettuce, mayonnaise and a center slice
Of beefsteak tomato.
The lettuce splayed, if you will,
In a Beaux Arts derivative of classical acanthus,
And the roast beef, thinly sliced, folded
In a multi-foil arrangement
That eschews Bragdonian pretensions
Or any idea of divine geometric projection
For that matter, but simply provides
A setting for the tomato
To form a medallion with a dab
Of mayonnaise as a fleuron.
And—as eclectic as this may sound—
If the mayonnaise can also be applied
Along the crust in a Vitruvian scroll
And as a festoon below the medallion,
That would be swell.

You mean like in the Cathedral St. Pierre in Geneva?

Yes, but the swag more like the one below the rosette
At the Royal Palace in Amsterdam.

You got it.
Next!

Seesaw

First Impressions

A ne'er-do-well but unhygienic

Unproductive and overshadowed but a minor talent

Shrill but gouged and trembling

Limited and irresponsible but an inveterate rhymester

Verbose but a splay-footed pigeon feeder

Ostentatious but a bleeder and subject to fits

Saving Graces

Delightfully garrulous yet a blowhard

Hilariously boorish yet a goon

Exquisitely devious yet untrustworthy

Artfully obsequious yet weepy and groveling

Explosively disagreeable yet a sore loser

Provocatively inarticulate yet mute

Like a demented child yet worrisome

Mordant, venomous yet in an overly critical way

Surprisingly obtuse yet unable to make fine distinctions

SEPTEMBER 13, 2001

"When you leave New York, you're not going anywhere,"
Del tells a bunch of customers leaving The Grange.
Leaving New York...? What a strange notion.
I'm out the door, too, uptown to teach another class.
Cabbies so annoyingly polite they throw me off my stride.
They're stopping at stop signs for Christ's sake.
On Commerce Street a building, narrow, tower-like—I
Never noticed it before—a great flaming rooftop grove
Of birches soaring in the wind. Phoenix...Phoenicity...
Is there such a word? Felix...Felicity—Anyway,
Something for this city to set its watch by.
Uptown early enough for another coffee, I stop
At the West End, keep a weak joke about Oswald Spengler
To myself, and ask Jay to translate what he's chalked up
On the slate board behind the bar. *Veni, Vidi, Velcro*:
"I came, I saw, I stuck around."

House of Xerxes

Here come those splendid Persians!
We were expecting fireworks
And here they are!
Short bows, long arrows, iron breastplates—
Nice fish-scale pattern on those breastplates.
Just the right beach touch, very decky.
Quivers dangling under wicker-worky shields,
A casual touch, that.
And those floppy felt caps
Make it all very wearable, very sporty.
Huge amounts of gold,
A killer-look feel
But it still says A Day at the Shore.

Now those bumping, thumping Assyrians.
A nice mix here: bronze helmets
Or plaited headgear.
Shields, spears, daggers,
The iron studs on those wooden clubs
A subtle retro bit.
And right on their heels the Bactrians!
A sort of butch-and-bitch combo,
Not tidy, not prim, almost
A dare-to-wear outfit.
And look at that headgear!
Whatever were they thinking?
And the bows, cane bows
Bringing back that beach scene scream.
Somebody's been smitten by cane.

Tromping right along: Scythians with a scowl!
Plenty of flounce and pout but somehow
It all spells powerhouse.
Stiff, pointed helmets and loose trousers,

Bows, daggers, battleaxes:
Just look at these ratty party boys.
Itchy and raw, apocalyptic but functional.
Takes us away from the beach look
But how can you not love them?

Look at these Sarangae!
Are we ready for this?
A lot of lavender, a lot of white and blue,
Colorama glamorama.
A little raggedy, a little trashy
Yet a narrow silhouette.
Narrow but masculine for sure.
Just what are these boys up to?

Oh, now how can you not love
These madcap Ethiopians.
Leopard skins and lion pelts,
Spear heads made of gazelle horns.
Now that is a new twist.
And who thought of this—body paint!
Half white chalk, half ochre.
The all-around mix and match
A big directional, indeed.

Check out the headgear!
A horse's scalp
Including ears and mane
For cryin' out loud.
Very jaunty, very focused.
Somebody pinch me!

Now, good grief, are we ready for the Libyans?
The brocade scaled back, thank god.
A big sulky leather look.
It's a bomber-jacket feeling.
I get a bomber-jacket feeling from this.

Javelins with burnt tips, daggers,
Minimal action gear but spiffy.

Marching, tromping right in,
What a welcome
For the Paphlagonian cuties!
Shields, spears, javelins and daggers—
Overloaded you might say, but
Why in heaven's name not?

Get a load of what's been done
With the traditional booties:
Halfway up the shin.
A booty and greave combo.
Now how cute is that?
And everyone agrees
Under those plaited helmets
Those Paphlagonians
Have the curliest hair in the world.

Here come the Thracians.
Fox-skin caps, fawn-skin boots, wooden helmets,
You just know how great
Their gorgeous garb makes them feel.

And right on their heels—The Pisidae!
Another wardrobe pick-me-up.
Bronze helmets shaped
Into the ears and horns of an ox.
What a way to say: Surprise!

A very jaunty crest,
Red cloth leggings,
Fashionable yet functional,
Smart but approachable,
Sporty in a tongue-in-chic sort of way.

You don't want to miss this!
Barefoot Sagartians, with lariats!
No optionals, nothing but lariats.
Now that is new.
No fashion fears here.
The total look flouncy, loose and extra large.

Turbaned Cyprians
With high high high high greaves!
Dangling daggers, billhooks!
Untreated ox-hide vests.
Something we'd want in our closet.
Lion, tiger, fox and ox: the full idiom.
Upbeat and very wearable,
A dose of novelty, a dose
Of frivolity—a definite smash.

They are having a good time up there.
Rough and raw yet a lot of flash.
Lavish, zippy, sleek.
Where is it all going?
An etude for today's world.
A dressy apocalyptic beach look.
A high-octane action look.
A premium blend of guts
And sass and imagination.
Feel the frenzy.

A big round of applause for the whole spectrum,
For a very big directional
That can't help but whip it up.
Who's able to take it all in?
Everyone's breathless.
Today we're making history.
We're raising cane.

THE ART OF RESTORATION

They eat off the same
commemorative plate.   Things
liven up when Miss Carmen   Figura
takes the stage gluttony of poets, the   language
of surly children is immediate, swipe of   eternal likened
to lichen they feed on stone and air but   prefer to wipe off
words with bread crust until only the   glow remains and they
see not their face reflected but the   expression on it how things
liven up when Miss Carmen Figura   her strawberries always look
wet, on juicy white glass her hands   as soft and slippy as peeled
pine, a little ruckus at her feet in the   whispery light rambunctious
Monks hurling firebombs chairs   chamberpots at each other a blue
underglaze iron red overglaze   masterful squiggle glow of a pop
-eyed five-claw dragon chasing   a flaming pearl Admit it, you can't
resist a woman who does her   research There you fumbled There
she snailed. What is a slow   rhyme to her is leaping magic to you
How she finger traced   and made the snail shell twirl and glow
it's easy to to to to   underestimate the hilarity of snails, that's
what slows them up   and around, Moonglow you can
write by, Revelation's   porcelain pop-light when
groggy in the dark you   holding this stepped on
a sleeping dog at   the top of the stairs.
lopsided   gift of Dr. and Mrs.

Acknowledgments

for Dale Devereux Barker

The artist and author wish to express their gratitude to the publications in which these collaborations originally appeared: "Particeps Criminis": *TransAtlantic Review*; "Disgruntled Lug": *Science and Wonder*; "Forbidden Rhymes": *Psychology Today*; "A Sable Figure Cloaked in Gloom Told Us This Hilarious Joke": *Psychological Digest*; "Killer Abstractions": *Modern Psychology*; "Poem Contaminated by Prepositions": *Times Literary Supplement*; "Elegy for the Split Infinitive": *New England Journal of Medicine*; "For the Development of the Split Infinitive": *The Wall Street Journal*; "To Our Esteemed Selves": *Humanities Quarterly*; "Oliver Happily Totals His Cadillac": *Dactyls on Parade*; "The Case Against the Gullible Pagans": *The Journal of Theological Studies*; "Our Friend, the Adverb": *Materials Management Weekly*; "Excellent Sonnet to a Nymph": *Hunters and Gatherers Quarterly*.

And our special thanks to *Haiku Annual* for a Special Mention Certificate for a Collaboration That Extols the Pleasures of Urban Life While Employing at Least Five Annoyingly Obscure Words and the Image of an Overturned Barrel of Olives on a Rain-glazed Cobblestone Street.

Envoy

An open book on the patio table,
Pages turning back and forth
As if it were reading itself
And lost its place.

That would be Force 1
On the Beaufort Scale, the gentlest:
Wind felt on face,
Smoke follows wind,
Thoughts follow smoke.

        . . .

Go, little book, glide
Down to where
Miles below, at my feet,
Dew-soaked cobwebs that rose
Overnight out of the pachysandra
Into a host of bright pavilions,
Shimmer and sag.

Through the drenched porch screen,
Through glistening, half-dead cedar,
Follow the downhill view
Of times trans-shifting,
Send a last slant of mist
Sailing off into the blue

To "that whiter island, where
        Things are evermore sincere:
Candor here, and luster there
                Delighting."

Here—Welcome to Putnam Valley
New York
Population: 9,500
Elevation: Infrequent

—and luster there,
Where pollen so fine it drifted
Through the screen, enaureoled
The cherry wood windowsill.

Swipe a few phrases as you go by,
Drawn here and there
With a fingertip, a few words
Scrawled in pollen and dust.

Make the most of the slightest breeze,
Coast over the heads
Of the innumerables, wave
To fretful bankers and clerks,
Tax collectors,
Traffic troopers,
Delirious archeologists,
Scriveners, car mechanics,
Mutilated saints, boggled messiahs,
And most of Wyoming.
Once again thank them
For giving me reason to insist:
Life is completely interesting.

Alight on a nose,
Flip a page or two,
Leave them wondering—
So much sail
For such a narrow hull—
How a butterfly
Always looks as if it's learning
How to—always looks
As if it's flying for the first time.

Float over the lowland skies
And washed-out roads,
The vague though uncontested
Boundaries of Apathy
And its neighboring realms.

Fold your wings (dilly
And dally) for a minute,
In the middle
Of what must be
Dereliction Junction.

Go to the louts and vagrants
In the marketplace,
The fish stall, or sprawled
On the greasy linoleum floor
In the mausoleum,
Or under the sooty roses
And mauled honeysuckle
Of the rank schoolyard grove.

Go with a little pity
And a little more disdain
To the abject sensualist who,
Pondering the tedious prospect
Of an afterlife, eyes
The spectral ascent of cigarette smoke
In a humid room
And suspects
Something incorrigible, perhaps
Sensual, indeed hopeful,
In how it climbs
Onto a ceiling cobweb.

Omni Animalium Post Coitum Marlboro.

Drop by the dusty palace if there's time.
Give my regards
To the Queen of Inertia, goddess
Of something or other.
Help her bestow some kind
Of achievement award
On Uncle Lethargy.

Linger a while
To celebrate
Ennui's birthday party.
Come on, let's hear it!
Happy Birthday, Little Ennui!
Bring a few gifts, amulets
To leave on the carcass
Of Complacency.

Salute the scribblers,
Advise them how
To infuse their themes
Of Languor and Negligence
With a ferocious splendor.
O Dissipation, Indifference,
A figuring forth,
A fury of resemblances, et cetera!
Abounding, abounding we will go!

Tell them at least
Paul Vioooooooooli,
A licensed poet,
Condemns their books
As a sizzling blank, devoid
Of what is sweet and right
And joyful, though he
Admires their acuity
On such matters as Indolence's
Exuding a stronger fragrance
Than Malaise.

Flick your wings
And set trees asway,
A whiff of exuberance
That will give
Wambly villagers
Yet another reason
To find sanctuary
In the nearest tavern.

You may as well,
While you're at it,
Make it a Force 10
On the Beaufort scale,
The most convincing.

Then before a furies' broth
Snatches striplings
Out of their boots,
Rabbits out of their warrens—

Before maidens collapse
And crones scramble
To bury their valuables
(And their cronies slyly note
Where they're digging),
Before harpies descend
On festivals and befoul the victuals—
Flee, little book!

Flee for all you're worth
Over the smeared maps of the world.
Find your own city in the night,
And the moment the air turns cool
Flow through an open window
In a black room.

Go to her in whose eyes
There is always
The moment the night air
Turns suddenly cool
With the newness of the day.

Go, little book, arrive
With the newness of the day
Hours before sunrise.

II For a February Songbook

Toward a February Songbook

A whirl of icy snow
Over fallen leaves could be a scrape
Or a caress, whisper or hiss.
A burning hiss or a buzz.
Dense oak, a few pine, a few rampike.
A nearly heart-shaped stone.
The one great beech, an eons-old nudge
From its sharkskin bark.
Low walls, neatly stacked then thrown
Into a sloppy heap the higher uphill they go.
Deadfall strewn willy-nilly
Like an abandoned game of pick-up sticks.
The thickly wooded land,
The very thought of the brutal work
It once took to clear it—Soon enough
The entire hillside will be buried
In greenery, the low stream will leap
Back into itself and guzzle away, but now,
Ah, now February is springtime for gray
And I'm at my light-hearted best.
Heart as light as a hornet's nest.

ALONG CANOPUS CREEK SOUTH OF SUNKEN MINE ROAD

1994

Sunlight above the wreckage,
As startling a gap in the woods
As grief or a collapsed building
Leaves on a city block.

Creek clogged, hillside impassable,
Criss-crossed with fallen oak and pine.
Ragged holes, root mounds, clumps of rock
And clay pried up like tin can lids.

The gale that tore through here last year,
Its roar stopped a moment ago.
A place fraught with immanent opposites,
A sense of aftermath and onslaught.

In the steep uphill glare,
The menace of a rearing dark;
In the looming hush, plunging masts
Of a devastated fleet.

Without the weight those great trees held,
The full sail of leaves and limbs,
With nothing for the wind to grab onto,
Only the dead were left standing.

Light Rain Falling on Deep Snow

The muttering of sedentary artisans
Hunched over desk and workbench
Two or three stories below
In the

        (I must have been half-listening for quite a while as I lay reading
in bed and, although I had dismissed other distractions and one or two
simmering regrets, I couldn't return to my book until I knew the origin
of that distant murmur. It's coming from below, from inside the house, I
thought, until—window slightly open to the night—I realized it was rain
falling soft and easy on deep snow. I put aside my book and turned off the
light, and listened a long time, for the sweet music it made was the newest
thing in the world to me. I felt a deep delight, a surprising gratitude.
A natural fact, simple, definite, arriving with an almost intimate flutter,
proved more pleasurable than anything I could imagine, and I wondered
if perhaps I had grown tired of imaginary things.)

    basement of the year:
A crowd of grubby, ancient artisans.
God knows what they're up to down there,
I'm lucky to have an inkling.
It's a fertile obscurity
And they mean to keep it that way.
Imagination, methinks, is a closed shop,
And even though I own the place,
I'm treated like an apprentice,
Never privy to how their nimble
Fingers can roll one smouldering drop
Of a cold night into a fat black pearl.
Hundreds of them, haughty grumps,
Finicky scribes and goldsmiths
Whose commands—Hey, runt!—
Keep me scurrying around:
Trim a wick, ladle out jewels
And metals, brush up gold dust,

Pass around a plate of facts,
A thimble full of whiskey.
Lug in more firewood,
Toss on another log,
A fresh cut willow to get the low
Flames rolling blue and yellow.
Fill an inkwell, trim a quill:
A buzzard quill for epitaphs,
An albatross for arrivals,
A goose for laughs, an eagle
For denials, a swan for
Invitations, a kiwi for regrets,
A condor for condolences,
A chickadee for threats,
And a red cardinal for what has flown,
For something dear and gone, not out
Of view but forever out of reach.

WRITTEN IN A TIME OF WORRY AND WOE

I stopped and leaned over the footbridge rail.
Far below, roaring by the library,
The stream plunged through deep winter with the force
That follows a spring thaw, re-enacting
In a short stretch its ever-varied course.
I watched it flow clear under clear black ice,
Churn frothy under gray, tunnel and swirl
Under snow, pool and spill, then slide over
And under overturned stumps and debris.
I watched until I thought: February—
The apex of the year, and felt so far
Above the sum of whatever I've known
Or seen or done that I couldn't care less
What I must have lost to feel so cold and free.

Acknowledgments

A month of twilights, laglight, fritterdusk. Withered plants, soggy bulbs, stubble. The Garden in February. Mold and tendrils, colorless scribbles dangling from a ripped-back carpet of matted leaves. Fresh hole in the frozen ground that looks like it was made by a pickaxe, a fang. Smeared dirt and frost, diamond slime. Paradise a child's notion. Paradise painted one stroke, one phrase, one glimpse at a time, whatever a lightning flare reveals of it. Blunderblink. An invitation. Mr. and Mrs. Dwindle. Request. Demand. The pleasure of your company, your antics, your fervor, your moodiness, your stolid numbing small-time solemnity, your contempt, your pig-headed pride, your carelessness, your squalling self.

PASTORALE

Paul Violi, volunteer, was on hand to enjoy
The day and encourage less experienced paddlers

> *Watch where the hell you're going!*
> *For the love of god, are you blind?*

And around the evening campfire offer the youngsters
The benefit of his knowledge and years

> *You guessed it, Fatso. If I had to*
> *Do it all over again, I'd be*
> *A friggin' diplomat.*

Before he retired for the night, stretched out
On a rock below the drifting stars,
Tracing their consternations
And recalling yet again a scene he thought
Illustrated the appeal good writing
Has for the discriminating reader,
A scene he had come across months ago
One clear blue February afternoon
When walking noiselessly in damp woods
He saw a fallen tree that, propped on rocks,
Had never hit the ground but hung dry
And hard, stripped of bark,
Deep-grooved and branchless,
Suspended like a bridge between nowheres.
And running beneath the length of it
A narrow mound of snow, melting but
Straight and sharp-edged in its shadow,
The only snow left on the hillside,
As blue as snow can get
And punctured by bird tracks
Which he pleasantly surmised

Whaddaya mean "surmised"? You think
I don't know what I'm looking at?

Were made by
A blue jay.

Poet and Cynic

If I'm hauling logs in muck and snow
He'll lie around and once in a while open
One eye to check on how I'm doing, then grab
A ridiculously long limb and drag
It triumphantly after me, making me feel
Like one of those profit-mad Corinthians
A mocking Diogenes chased around
The marketplace, rolling a cracked barrel
At their heels. But this toss-and-fetch, uphill
And down, an indefatigable Sisyphus,
The gleeful futility of it, all
Afternoon if I were game and didn't want
To do anything else but go inside
And scribble and scrawl, scribble and scrawl…

INKLING IN A FLURRY

Nature loves to hide, Heraclitus noted,
Leaving others to quibble over the meanings
Maybe camouflaged in the word *nature*
Until the sense and then the ink squirm
Out of all the words and letters, inkling
Into the shadows that on the wide bright
Pavement shift and sway like light on water,
Continuously rewritten, shadows
Of limbs and branches and a faster one
Cast by a circling hawk, which keeps the mouse
Hunched on the roadside waiting for a flurry
Of dead leaves to blow over him before
He jumps in, scrambles for all he's worth,
Un—except for that crazy grin—detectable.

Panorama

"My films never end, they never have
a simple solution."

Fellini, you must be alive at this hour,
Behind the scenes, calling the shots.
While I'm waiting behind the wheel,
Trying to decide whether to let the car
Warm up more or get going before
The roads get worse, this winged zero
Soars out of the night snow
And (Extreme Close-up) slams me in the face.
Nice touch, Maestro!
Ten minutes ago I was sailing
Through class, throwing out what I know
As if bailing out a boat.
Now what am I supposed to do?
Stare out at this dull town
Now that for no reason, not even
Mere weariness, any faith or delight
Has been blown away like ashes
In the wild and brilliant snow
That has left Bloomfield vacant
(Extreme Long Shot), closed it down
But for one pizza shop, a fluorescent blank
(Medium Shot) across the avenue, so
Picture perfect it seems fake,
Except for the waitresses and waiters
(Medium Close-up) in their black skirts
And pants and white blouses and T-shirts
Who stare like mourners into the night
Until one has sense enough to toss
A piece of crust at the one
Wiping the lid (Extreme Close-up)
Of the giant oven and another flicks

A spoonful of flour at a waitress
Who scoops up a pile with both hands
And (Wide Shot) splashes him down
(Close-up) before he twirls a floppy lasso
Of dough across the marble counter
And the air (Wide Shot) blooms
With doughballs and napkins, dish rags
And flour (Medium Close-up) and out
The door they fly in whiteface
And run and jump, dance and tumble
In each other's arms and the whirling
Air (Wide Shot) as I roll slowly
By them (Tracking Out), simple as that.

To Himself

You watch one more crow drop
Out of the overcast
Onto a patch of snow
And stand with others
In a circle,
Far enough away
To look like a jagged crown,
Close enough not to.
 Either way enough
 To make you play
 A little something
 On your violio.

Your steps don't leave
A trace on the hard path,
The ground sounds hollow
Beneath your feet,
In frozen mud the deep day-
Or week-old tracks—
boots, sneakers, paws—
Are all headed one way…
 The sort of thing
 That could make you
 Snap a string
 On your violio.

You look like one
Whom time has surprised,
Though the perfect sense
Of what is final,
The inmost view
From behind the past,
Beyond the long slope,
The frost and tall grass,

Is not new to you:
      You've played along
      With it once or twice
      On your violio.

Tuft and scrub still bent
In the direction
The wind last blew,
You plunk, you hum
A few notes,
You try to catch a tune
That's already flown
Right through you
With a sound
As quick as daybreak
And as light
And hard as bone.
You're on your own,
      With a little something
      You can play all day,
      Strum or hack away
      On your violio.

Brief Lives…

Joseph Boruwlaski, born in Poland in 1739,
Lives to be almost 98, a record for a dwarf.
He considers Poland his "cradle"
And, eventually, England his "nest."
He is buried in Durham Cathedral
Under a slab marked JB.
In St. Mary-the-Less Church
A memorial tablet says he faced changes
In fortune with cheerful resignation.
His childhood nickname is Jou-Jou.
Orphaned at nine, he is taken in by aristocrats.
At 15, in the care of Countess Humeicka,
He tours the courts of Europe.
Gavines teaches him to play the violin;
Count Orginski, Grand General
Of Lithuania, teaches him music;
Angelini, ballet master, the art of dancing.
Empress Maria Theresa takes a great liking to him.
A young Marie Antoinette gives him a diamond ring.
All the ladies love to hold and fondle him,
But he yearns for Isalina,
A lady-in-waiting who loves him in return.
When he refuses to renounce her, the Countess
Expels him from her home.
He marries Isalina.
He comes under the protection of King Stanislaus II,
Who gives him the title of Count.
He reaches his maximum height at age 30: 3′ 3″.
Noblemen friends convince him that,
Being handsome, witty and a bit of a huckster,
He could support his wife by exhibiting
Himself and playing the violin.
He and Isalina tour Europe, arriving in London in 1782.
He always presents himself as a gentleman, never an oddity.

Georgina, Countess of Devonshire, befriends him.
Her husband gives him an embroidered suit and silver sword.
The Prince of Wales persuades him to publish his memoirs.
One surviving copy contains an anonymous comment,
Calling him "a duodecimo edition of humanity,"
And a sketch of him playing a tune
Before the Sultan of Turkey, three "full blown
And highly developed beauties"
Of the harem, and three gigantic guards.
He tours the British Isles, playing his own compositions.
In Edinburgh, the Scots, finding Boruwlaski hard
To pronounce, call him "Barrel of Whiskey."
The Duke and Duchess of Marlborough become his patrons.
Tactful hosts usually place a stack of books
On his chair before guests arrive for dinner.
His wife and children desert him.
Long after she dies he still complains about his wife,
How when he annoyed her she would put him
On a high shelf and leave the room.
The actor Stephen Kemble (who
At 476 pounds played Falstaff
Without stuffing) becomes a dear friend.
Both of them die on the same day.
He travels often in his life, as far as Lapland
And Nova Zembla, where fascinated natives
Keep him awake day and night,
And in their songs thank the sun (which they
Politely decline to believe is a star)
For allowing them to see this man.

For It Feels Like February 29th or 30th

For we were made to reach for things.
For imagination extends life.
For our reach must exceed our grasp.
For in confinement imagination thrives.
For The Book of the Month Club selection
Has finally arrived.
For it is *The Life of Jeffrey Hudson*.
For it is a February Classic.
For a wondrous life he made.
For he flourished in confinement.
For he was a champion who scoffed at restriction.

For at age nine, though scarcely 18 inches tall,
He was gracefully proportioned.
For he was a page to Duke Edward.
For at a banquet he leaped out of a pie
Placed before Queen Henrietta Maria.
For she was delighted and adopted him on the spot.

For he was made captain of cavalry.
For he was called Strenuous Jeffrey.
For he was tireless and heroic.

For firing from horseback
He killed his opponent in a duel.
For he was captured by Dunkirkers and imprisoned.
For upon his release
He was found to have grown taller.

For he was imprisoned by Turkish pirates.
For when freed from captivity
He had grown a foot taller.

For after the Restoration he was pensioned.
For as an accused conspirator in the Popish Plot
He was again imprisoned and again released.
For shortly thereafter he died
At the age of 63 at the height of 3 foot 9.

EXTENDED SHORTAGES

I must remind you how serious I've become,
Almost grave (though still immensely likeable).

Love threatens to carry me off
Like a dancer in a trash-heap storm.

A counterweight! I need a counterweight.
I read history late into the night,
A scavenger, loading up
On high deeds and disillusionment,
Treachery and hope, until I am unable
To hop over a footnote.

An ashtray crowning a stack of Gibbon,
A scotch and soda atop the King James,
Eventually a whiff of pity comes my way,
Not for me but for that sad Titan,
The dim-witted one who has to bear
The weight of heaven and earth,*
Gravity and exhilaration, on his back.
Then I can snooze, snicker at my own
Grief and short-comings and snooze.

When I wake and rise and slowly dress
with dust motes whirling madly about me
In that lovely solemn light, I do not risk
Even thinking about you until I feel
The weight of all I recall sink to my feet
And then in a bow to Philetus,**
I reach for my shoes.

*5.972 sextillion metric tons.

**Philetus of Cos, poet, teacher, famed for his love lyrics,
admired by Ovid and Propertius, tutor to Ptolemy of
Philadelphus, so small he had to wear lead shoes
Lest in the desert wind he be blown away.

Thief Tempted by the Grandeur of February

Wake up! I can't wait to tell you
How much I learned in my sleep.
And though I remain somewhat modest
And completely charming,
I have indeed changed.

Do you know that taxidermy students
Begin with a mastodon
And end by stuffing a flea?
And as for poetry, it's easy
And impossible—like stealing from yourself.

Do you know that whenever a weatherman
Grows alarmingly unpredictable,
As long as he retains
A bit of modesty and charm,
He's promoted to astronomer?

And that like an astronomer in the mist,
I am coaxed onward, in love
With the blessings of sleep,
The lustre of sleeplessness, more and more
Aware of how serious I've become
Because of you—serious
And yet somehow remarkably pleasant.

The beauties of the night, I already know
What it's like to feel cold
And beautiful hair slide through my hands.
Beyond the edge of forgetfulness
Or the last of a fine rain,
A few memories flare
And sputter in a final appeal.
What once seemed true,

What once seemed wrong,
I let them disappear, blown away
By a caress, a spray of light here
And there across slick, wide avenues.
Distant pleasures, distant strife,
I now can say, modestly
But not without significant charm,
I know the errors of my life.